The Complete Guide to Real Estate
Lease Options
And
Owner Financing
A Reference Guide for Buyers and Sellers

By
J. Mark Eason

ISBN: 9781520301761
Second Edition © 2016

TABLE OF CONTENTS

CHAPTER 1:
THE ESSENCE OF THE DEAL

To some this will become your "bible", the ultimate reference for buying or selling a home or property. For others this will simply be a book to help them understand certain aspects of life and business. As a result, you will have a better understanding of how things work in life and how to use your interpersonal skills to create opportunities.

Opportunities abound in America, if you're willing to look for them, be tenacious, and understanding of your fellow man or woman. I am not about to suggest that the solutions presented in this book are the only options available. Nor am I claiming this book should replace common sense and the need to consult with a lawyer, CPA or realtor. My intent with this book is to give you knowledge, and knowledge is power.

For hundreds of years in this country, Americans have demonstrated a spirit that included both independence and reliance. We trust our own independent abilities to succeed but still rely on the honest support of others in order to gain success in this life. This is the fundamental spirit that has shaped the country to become as it is today.

Unfortunately, because we often choose to believe a vast quantity of negative media, we often convince ourselves that we can no longer trust one another and that we need intermediaries or a "go between" to deal with each other in today's world. These intermediaries or "go betweens" are lawyers, realtors, accountants, bankers, mortgage companies, etc. These professions or services have their place in society and have contributed significantly over the years to its success, but they do not replace human interaction. Sadly, many of us have allowed them to do so.

The vast majority of people in this country and in the world want the same thing out of life. They want to be able to live a good life, provide for their families and establish a home where they can feel safe and comfortable. People need and want to trust one another. It is a fundamental "glue" that holds societies together. It is particularly important that we trust each other in business deals or commerce transactions. Simply put, no written contract is stronger than one human being's commitment to another. In this day of lawyers and lawsuits this may sound "old fashioned", but it is a fundamental factor in all transactions between people, regardless of all the written and legal assurances, people must TRUST one another.

I grew up in Texas where one hundred to one hundred million dollar deals are made every day on the basis of a handshake. I am not suggesting that this is the way you do business or negotiate the deal on your house or property. It is, however, the essence or the most important ingredient of what I am saying. Buying or leasing a home with a lease option or owner financing will require that the parties involved trust one another to do what is agreed upon and recorded in legal documentation. You may want to engage a lawyer or realtor to review these documents or even construct them, but essentially it all boils down to a fundamental agreement between people. This is a key ingredient. You must be able to establish a rapport with the seller.

This is not a book on how to buy a home, per se. I am not a real estate professional or lawyer. This book is specifically about how to buy and sell property using the techniques of lease options and owner financing. My expertise comes from many years of experience. What I give here should not be considered as "legal advice". This book has been written to give you a basis from which to work. In other words, it gives you knowledge and information.

THE BUYER

Any time you enter into a legally binding contract, such as a lease option or owner financing, you must use common sense and be prudent in your activities. I strongly recommend that you seek the advice of an attorney before signing anything. However, do not let the professionals make the final decision for you. In the end, it will be your decision and many times it will be based on things other than legal documents. Often it will be based on "gut" feelings, or feelings from the heart. I think those components must figure into the mix because ultimately, these deals are between human beings.

This book is written as a general reference. Different states and counties have different laws regulating the sale and purchase of property. I have purchased property in California, Texas, Colorado and Florida using the techniques outlined in this book and I have found the laws to be very similar. However, that may or may not be the case in your state and county. I suggest you check with the county property office for information. Although, they cannot give you legal advice, they can give you the general rules that govern such sales.

As you start this journey, remember, the United States has very specific laws that provide equal opportunity to housing for everyone regardless of race, creed, color or religion. I will explain this more in detail later in the book, but want you to have this fact in mind as you start your search for your home.

Making the Dream Come True

The dream of owning your own home can be a reality regardless of your income, station in life or credit. Through this book you will learn how to select and negotiate a lease option (also called lease purchase, purchase option or rent to own) and acquire owner financing. I have purchased or sold numerous properties using this method and have been able to buy premium property, sometimes with little or no money down. In all cases, I have generated equity in the property even before I purchased it by negotiating a lease option. You will benefit directly from my experience. By using these techniques, I have never had my credit checked or paid points or excessive closing costs.

I purchased my first house using this method when I was twenty-nine years old and sold it one year later at a price fifty percent higher than what I paid! By the way, when negotiating the purchase of this house, I had no credit whatsoever. I had rented from the owners for over a year and they trusted me. I did not exploit that trust, but used it to the best advantage. They got what they wanted (needed) and so did I.

This home purchased utilizing the program described in this book was on a beautiful half acre of land in Central Florida. This custom home came completely furnished with all the amenities including a fabulous indoor heated swimming pool. It even included a Cub Cadet☐ tractor-mower. The owners had originally wanted to just rent the property. I offered to rent it and then buy it for a pre-negotiated price. They had their own personal reasons for selling their dream home (the wife had designed the home on the back of a paper bag). But, I didn't approach them with an attitude of arrogance or as a "shark", but with a profound respect for the beauty and comfort of their home, not their house. We ended up having a wonderful long-term relationship and we eventually purchased additional rental property they owned. We in turned sold this property under lease option/owner financing program and made a nice profit on those transactions as well. At all times, each person's personality was at play. It is imperative that you understand that people don't just trust you with their property. In many cases, they are entrusting you with dreams.

A few years later, I accepted a new job on the West coast in Northern California. We sold our Florida home for 50% more than we had financed it for a year earlier. It took us about two weeks to sell and there was no negotiation over price.

You, too, can buy the home of your dreams. And in spite of what you may think, you won't be limited to buying some cheap "fixer upper". .

Once we started looking for homes in Northern California, we decided to apply the same system in California that we had used with such success in Florida. We looked for properties that were listed "For Sale". If we liked the property, we would offer the owner, sometimes through a realtor, to purchase the house under a lease option/owner financing arrangement.

We found a custom redwood house one block from the Pacific Ocean that had been listed for sale for about six months. The home was beautifully crafted with custom redwood cabinets, stair railings and wall paneling. There were skylights and balconies, a charming wood stove that heated the entire upstairs, two car garage, washer, dryer, refrigerator and a breathtaking view of the Pacific Ocean,

The house was being sold through a local realty company. Fortunately they had a realtor who was flexible and understood the need of her customers and was willing to accept an eventual, not immediate, commission as a workable solution. We offered the owners (unfortunate, but not unusual, involved in a divorce), a lease option/owner financing proposal. They were eager to accept our terms. It meant an immediate cash infusion for them via the lease and a guaranteed purchase under the lease option. They were delighted with the offer. The realtor had to wait a year for her commission, until the actual financing (owner in this case) was consummated. If you can find this kind of realtor, treat them like gold. They *understand* the process and are willing to wait for their compensation.

We sold the home about six years later. Because of the extremely low California market, we didn't have as much equity as we had anticipated, but it was enough to give us a negotiating position on our new home in Denver and enable us to buy a new business.

Our Denver lease option/owner-financing plan was extremely favorable and at the same time a fiasco. That may sound like conflicting terms, but in reality we were able to parley the existing and, fortunately negotiable lease option into a fabulous new house in an exclusive community at 8,000' overlooking the city of Denver. After a year of leasing with option, the owners of the property decided that they had a much higher value of the property than the appraiser. We were unwilling to pay beyond the appraised price for the house, which we felt was fair and equitable, so instead we opted to move to a condo in the mountains. We had saved a small sum of money to use as a down payment on the original deal or on another home, if the opportunity arose. To make a long story short, the manager of the condo offered us an opportunity to build a custom home in one of the most prestigious neighborhoods in Denver. The Denver housing economy was at its lowest in years, and developers were willing to cut any kind of deal. We had a good record, a "small" amount of cash (we got 95% financing!) and the opportunity to build our dream house. So, at some level, the lease option/ owner financing deal propelled us into our dream home. We were able to secure "conventional" financing for this property and lived six years under the umbrella of a legitimate mortgage.

A few years later we sold our business in Denver. The plan was to live off the residuals of the sale for a few years while we decided where to go and what to do. Unfortunately, within a few months, the buyer of our business defaulted on our loan and we were thrown into the position "fight or flight." We decided to do both. Thanks to a friend in Florida, we were offered a six-month consulting contract, which would pay for our living and lawyer expenses. Instead of selling our home in Denver, we continued to rent it for ten years and then offered financing to the current tenants. Unfortunately, they were unable to afford the house. It had simply appreciated out of their price range, so we sold it conventionally for $575,000. We had purchased the home for $349,000.

Once in Florida, we were fortunate to be able to rent a beautiful townhouse on a golf course from a friend. During this time, we started looking for a house that we could to buy, that we afford and that was located in an area that was sure to grow rapidly over the years. We had very limited resources at the time, considering our fiscal predicament. After a few months, we found an absolutely beautiful and functional home located on a key off the west coast of Florida, which was listed, for rent by the owner. Utilizing the methods outlined in this book, we approached the owner with a lease option/owner financing proposal. The owners were at first intrigued and then thrilled to lock in a five-year lease and a sales agreement at the same time. We locked in a price, which, personally, I felt at the time, was a bit excessive, but we trusted the future to "iron things out."

As it turned out, the purchase price after five years was $310,000. When the first term ended, we didn't feel secure with this price and asked to lease, under the same terms, including purchase price for another five years. The decision the owners had to make was to give up a lucrative income and purchase promise or start all over again. They agreed to our proposal. Then a strange thing happened. At about two years into the second lease term, the owners said they would sell the house, now, for $265,000. That was a significant drop in the original price. At that point, we were intrigued enough to get a professional appraisal of the property.

The property appraised at $375,000! Needless to say we immediately began the purchase process through a local mortgage company. In spite of our checkered credit past, the loan went through without a hitch. We were thrilled and the owners were happy. Since they only owed $110,000 on the property, they were ecstatic to receive a very large cash return on the property.

This house was a three story modern design overlooking the Gulf of Mexico. It was located on Siesta Key, one of the most beautiful island beaches in the United States. We estimate this house to currently have a value in excess of $700,000.

The Harder You Work, the Luckier You Get

The thrill of owning your own home is hard to put into words. Just imagine no more landlords, no more rent and lousy, expensive rental property and no more arrogant lending agents looking into every detail of your life.

As you begin the process of finding and implementing a lease option/owner financing deal, you will be challenged with many obstacles. Some may be new to you or involve dealing with types of people who have a different "perspective" of the world than you. At all times, it is essential that you remain positive and impervious to issues that may be or appear or appear to be personal in nature. You have to remain above any seemingly personal attacks or insults in order to succeed. Remember, this is a win/win situation. Some people are very suspicious of other people and/or very negative because of events in their own lives. You must be prepared to deal with these people and succeed.

Obviously, there is nothing "magical" or "mystical" about buying a home or property. However, you must be prepared to achieve the best, to not "short change" yourself, or let others do it to you. You must supplement your skill and expertise with a positive and winning attitude. Review the following list of keys to being a successful person:

1.   Decide that you will pay whatever price and make whatever effort is needed, within your personal guidelines or goals,

2.   Decide that you will focus on ideas of good fortune; that you will never again think of bad luck as either normal or inevitable, as somehow a part of your particular fate.

3.   Decide that even if there were a thing as "inevitable fate," you can overcome it. There is still the power within you to choose what you will do about it and create your world from within.

4.   Decide that you are not a victim of anything. No matter what your problems or how confused your way, or how heavy your load, the laws of life rush to your aid when you consciously believe in them and you invoke them. They work best when you recognize them and, in a sense command them.

5.   The successful people are the ones who seem to get most of the "good luck." Sometimes they have been born into such an environment. But more often, the successful person has chosen to create a habit of getting the edge on whatever he or she is doing. The harder and smarter you work, the "luckier" you become

6.   Be absolutely positive. Decide that for two weeks, at least, you will monitor your self-talk. Talk POSITIVE to yourself and others. .

7.   Eliminate scary headlines quickly from your mind. Unless you are going to help personally, don't stress over the disaster in the news. This is not selfish. Think and be positive.

8.   Decide to give yourself better "breaks." Learn to snatch extra minutes during the day for a little study, meditation or work.   The most complex and intimidating task can be broken down into manageable components. Identify and complete the task one step at a time.

9.   Praise your good fortune. Like applause to a singer or water to a plant, recognition and praise of your life tend to multiply them. But if you say when some disappointment or inconvenience comes along, "Just my luck," you are claiming for your very own that which you do not want. Gratitude is one of the strongest steps toward good fortune. Remember that in a theater, if you do not applaud the entertainment given you, you will not receive more, i.e., an encore. By the same token, appreciation anywhere is quite likely to attract or create appreciation in return.

10.   Call everything good. If an offer is rejected, either re-negotiate or move on. The next property will be a better deal. When you find someone who will listen to your offer, praise your luck. Don't say, "Well, it's about time I had a break." Such remarks articulate your belief in your usual bad luck. There's a far difference between praising your good fortune and noting it as unusual in a cynical fashion.

11.   You will be tested and tried in the matter, especially as you negotiate for a home or property. As you praise your good fortune and it begins to grow, you become aware that you are dealing with a genuine force about which we know all too little. Everything will not go your way. However, if you remain true to the principle of the ethical offer, eventually you will succeed.

12.   Life is like riding an elevator in a tall building. At which floor do you get off to transact your life's business? If you prefer the cellars of the world, you have a long, painful way ahead of you.

13.   Even if yours is a respectable life "of quiet desperation," as Thoreau once said of all humanity, you must shed the untamed belief in confusion and set about cultivating the patterns in which things come out well.

14.   Think up ways to give more at every turn. It is truly astonishing how much time most of us spend trying to give less and less, while we hope for more and more! It doesn't make sense. The only place we should give less should be in cutting down the time we spend in dissatisfaction, fatigue, and negative talk. Make your extras those of value, appreciation, fun, and beauty. Then, as your momentum gathers and propels you forward without so much conscious effort and fuel, you begin to enjoy your reward.

You must put yourself in line with that which you desire. If you wanted a suntan, you would understand quite clearly that you must place yourself where the sun can shine on you. This is a good metaphor, for the sun shines on the just and the unjust, its rays reach everything and everybody. Just so with all natural forces, they operate for anyone who operates them. Remember, you cannot control other people's behavior....you can only control how YOU react to it.

FOR BUYERS AND SELLERS - LEASE OPTIONS DEFINED

OK, what is a lease option? A lease is defined as a contract granting use or occupation of property during a specified period in exchange for a specified rent. An option is defined as the exclusive right, usually obtained for a fee, to buy or sell something within a specified time at a set price. Therefore, a lease option is, simply, a rental agreement with a built in "option" that allows for the purchase of a property at a specific price during a specific period of time. Most lease options, and all the ones I have negotiated, included financing by the owner at the conversion or end of the lease. Interest rates, down payments, if any, and the terms of the financing are "locked in" at the time the lease is negotiated and signed. Also, a portion of the monthly lease payment is applied to the down payment when (and if) the lease is converted to a purchase.

Other lease options will require the lessor to provide their own financing at the end of the lease. Even if the owner is unwilling to finance at the end of the lease; under the lease option there will a pre-determined price for the property established with the lease option. Other facets of lease options can also apply such as down payment and a portion of the rent going toward a down payment. In one real life scenario, I agreed to acquire my own financing at the end of the lease, but agreed to a purchase price of $289,000. After sixty months of leasing, the house was appraised at $412,000. Financing was no problem. I had lenders falling over themselves to finance a home with over $123,000 of equity.

Another advantage of a lease option is that during the term of the lease, the owner is your landlord and must maintain the property, pay the taxes and maintain all necessary insurance. However, during this time, you have "locked in" your purchase price. Any appreciation that occurs during the term of the lease is yours.

OWNER FINANCING DEFINED

OK, we've defined lease options, what does owner-financing mean? Instead of selling their home for cash, owners can choose to finance the home under an agreement for deed. They can do this regardless of whether or not they owe money on the property. In fact, it usually doesn't make any difference whatsoever whether there is a balance due on the property since the original mortgagor remains personally liable if the buyer defaults (fails to make the monthly payments). Since the original mortgagor (the seller) remains liable in the event of default, the mortgagee's (lending institution's) consent is not required for a sale subject to a mortgage (agreement for deed). The only exception to this rule is if the original mortgage contains a "due on sale" clause. This means, that as a condition of the original loan, the seller must pay the mortgage in full if the property is sold. These clauses only "kick" in when the purchase of the property is imminent; you will need to verify whether or not it exists. If it does, the seller is probably prevented from negotiating an agreement for deed or at least from recording such an agreement. If the agreement cannot be recorded, you can still purchase the property as outlined in this book, but there are significant additional risks involved. I do not recommend that you attempt to "go around" the due on sale clause. I suggest that there are ways to still purchase the property. If the lease option/owner financing deal can't be disclosed because of a due on sale clause, then you must do the ethical thing and work with the lender. They do have room, and sometimes and incentive to negotiate. I have included Title 12 -Chapter 13 - Sec. 1701j-3. – Of the U.S. Code Preemption of due-on-sale prohibitions in the reference section. I have also included Section 5402 – Definitions. Please read these sections carefully.

The sales price, down payment, interest rate, and term of the contract are all negotiable. In many cases, owners do not want a large down payment because of tax considerations, they are anxious to sell, they are looking for long-term monthly income or you have already "paid" your down payment (or a portion of it) through your lease option.

ADVANTAGES OF HOME OWNERSHIP

So why bother to buy a home in the first place? Here is a short list of advantages to home ownership:
• Taxes - One of the most obvious reasons for financing a home is the reduction of your income tax. All of your interest payments on your mortgage (agreement for deed) should be deductible. This can mean a significant difference in the taxes you pay. None of your rent is deductible.

• Appreciation - Almost without fail, houses appreciate in value. That means each year they are worth more than the previous year. As you reduce the balance of your mortgage, the value of your home increases. The difference between what you owe and what your house is worth is called equity.

•   Security - "A man's (or woman's) home is his (or her) castle". A home represents security. Your monthly payment won't change at the whim of your landlord. It is yours to remodel, to decorate and to landscape as you chose, to your taste. Unless you live in a neighborhood that has covenants (certain rules for homeowners) you can do what you like with your home to enhance its appearance and value.

•   Pride and Status - Home ownership puts you in a different category from renters. There is pride associated with owning your own home and it increases your self-esteem and status.

Let's review what we've learned so far:

1)   You can own your own home utilizing lease option and owner financing.

2)   Be prepared to have a positive and successful attitude. Study the steps to being a successful person. You will benefit significantly from this attitude when negotiating a purchase or a sale.

3)   A lease option is, simply, a rental agreement with a built in option to purchase the property, at a specific price during a specific period of time under specific terms.

4)   Instead of selling their home for cash, owners can choose to finance the home for you under an agreement for deed.

5)   Trust is the essence or the most important ingredient in negotiating a lease option/owner financing.

6)   Home ownership can provide a tax advantage, pride of ownership, appreciation, equity, security and status

CHAPTER 2
FINDING THE RIGHT PROPERTY

Where you start will depend on your particular situation. Let's assume you are currently renting and would like to purchase a home. The first thing you will want to do is find the general area or neighborhood where you want to live. If you have children in school, consider a location where the best schools are located or that is in your current school district. If children are not a consideration now, will they be in the future? Remember, you are going to make a long-term commitment. Plan accordingly. The three most important criteria for the purchase of property are "location, location, location". This is the simple truth.

You will need to determine how much you can pay for a monthly lease, down payment and mortgage.

The first place to look is in the classifieds of the newspaper (See Figure 1). Look for listings first under lease options, rent to own, lease purchase or for sale by owner. Some newspapers carry these headings, and some do not. If these headings are available, check there first. Owners or Realtors under these headings are looking for an arrangement similar to what is described in this book. Use the "Tracking Sheet" in Figure 2 to track your search and help you stay organized.

Even if the terms are spelled out in the ad, still call and ask about the house, its general location, and the terms offered. Record the call in your notebook. Don't be intimidated, but don't be pushy either. You are usually dealing with homeowners and not professionals. Owners tend to have an emotional attachment to their property, and you will need to be sensitive to that. If the property is listed with a Realtor, skip it until you've read the section on that topic.

A word of caution: Some owners (usually Realtors themselves) will want an option payment in advance or want you to buy the option. Sometimes this payment is called earnest money, offer to purchase or a binder. Although this is a perfectly legitimate practice, I do not recommend it. This is an unnecessary expense and it may or may not apply to the sales price of the property. Approximately 50% of buyers do not exercise their options, for one reason or another. So, if you decide not to exercise your purchase option, you'll probably forfeit any payment of this type. If this is a requirement for the option, this is probably not a viable property.

A **PROPERTY TRACKING SHEET** should include the following:

Property Owner (Contact Name)   Sales Price
Address   Monthly Lease Rent Amount
City and/or Neighborhood   Description of Property

Don't be discouraged if there are no listing or if the listings are totally unreasonable or out of your range. If there are no headings like the ones listed, you can look under house for sale and for rent or lease in the general area where you want to live.

Use the same advice mentioned above when calling about these ads. Even though the house is listed for sale, the owner could have lots of reasons to consider a lease option. They could be transferred and need to move, or have already purchased another home. When calling to ask the owner about the property, ask if they would consider leasing the house with an option to buy. If it is listed for rent or lease, ask if they would consider selling the house under a lease option and agreement for deed.

I have found houses by looking for those listed both as rentals and for sale. What you will find is that many houses listed by the owner for rent or lease have actually previously been on the market for sale. For some reason the owner was unable to move the property and decided to rent it instead.

Another option for finding a suitable property is to drive around in the neighborhoods you have chosen. Look for "For Sale by Owner", "For Rent" and "For Lease" signs. Write down the information such as address and phone number and call the owner as outlined above. The key is to identify, as many properties as you can that you consider suitable by virtue of location and price. Now work your way through the list. For those who express an interest, make an appointment to visit with them at the property. Obviously, these are the most likely prospects and could provide you with the opportunity you are looking for.

The Internet
Another way to find a house for sell or lease by owner is through the Internet. If you are connected, go to your web browser and search for "houses for sale by owner", "lease options" or "owner financing". My browser identified over seventy-two thousand possible matches. These properties were located throughout the United States and the world. Some excellent sites are http://www.owners.com and www.fsbo.com. It is very possible that a property compatible with your criteria is available. If you are not Internet literate, don't worry. The other methods listed will work fine. This is just one more resource available to you, but it's a good one. Another place to look is Craigslist under real estate.

Although the Internet is THE place today to find home listings, please never ASSUME it's the only source. All the other sources listed in this book are as valid as any other. I recommend that you combine all sources to find the best deals.

Your Current Residence
One of the best places to look for an opportunity is in your own back yard. If you are currently renting and like where you live, approach the owner about the possibility of buying the house. If you have lived there for a while, you will most likely have developed some sort of track record of payments, and therefore trust. All the criteria discussed in this book would apply. It never hurts to ask. You could be already living in your dream home. Remember, rent is not deductible on your income tax and no matter how long you rent, you never build any equity in the property.

Your Image and Demeanor

In most cases, you will be dealing with individuals and not companies or professional Realtor. Your demeanor, or the way a person behaves or acts is very important to the prospective seller/lessor. They are looking for someone they can trust. You will be asking them to give you an opportunity to buy their home or property and offering them an opportunity to make a lot of money from the sale and/or leasing their home.

In order to do that that you must show that:

a) You are a trustworthy person, who is sincere about buying their house,

b) You have the resources necessary to make monthly payments; this means that you have a good, stable job (or jobs if married), and,

c) That you are not some "slick" operator after their money and property.

Always dress appropriately when visiting properties. It is important to create an image of honest, dependable, respectable people. Don't wear the clothes you use to mow the lawn or clean the house. Husband and wives should go together.
In review, we:

1.   Look for opportunities in the classified ad headings "for sale by owner" or "lease   option" or "rent to own".

2.   Look for a house in your chosen neighborhood and at the price you want that is listed for sale or for rent. The owner may be willing to listen to a proposal.
3.   Drive around in selected neighborhoods looking for appropriate properties.

4.   "Surf' the Internet under "houses for sale by owner", or selected web sites that cater to homes for sale by owner.

5.   Remember that owners have an emotional attachment to their properties.

6.   If you are currently renting a house, consider making a lease option/owner financing proposal to the owner.

7.   Present a professional and trustworthy image. Spouses and partners should look together

CHAPTER 3
NEGOTIATING LEASE OPTIONS AND OWNER FINANCING

In most cases, it will be your responsibility to "educate" the seller about the prospect of lease option and owner financing. Rarely have I met people who knew much about this opportunity. However, when I explained about the benefits and protection for the owner, they became interested.

We have already defined a lease option. Sometimes, it is called something else like "rent to own" or "lease purchase". For the purposes of this book, we will assume that they are all the same things. I have included, in the appendix, a sample lease option form for you to review. Standard forms are available at most office supply stores and can be modified or rewritten to suit your purpose. Actually, the option can be simply added to the lease as an addendum. An addendum is defined as something added or to be added. If the seller already has a lease form, use it with an addendum attached that describes the terms of the lease option and possibly the owner financing. You should be very clear in describing the option so there is no misunderstanding later on. Do not trust your memory or the seller's memory. Put it in writing.

Leases can have a variable term. In other words, they can be six months, one year, two years, etc. in length. Although the term is negotiable, most people will want a one to two year commitment in order to feel secure about the deal. In some cases, the longer the lease, the better it is for the buyer for the following reasons:

a)   It gives you more time to accrue or build a down payment,

b)   If you have a portion of the rent going toward the down payment, time will allow you reduce the amount of cash required, and

c)   The house or land will continue to appreciate, even while you rent.

So what should the lease look like and how do you negotiate terms? Essentially, you will use a standard lease form that contains all the common language associated with leases. The owner or lessor may have their own form that they will require you to use or they may ask you to come up with one. I suggest that you use a form that is standardized and that is found at office supply stores. These forms are designed to be legal and you can modify the language in them if it isn't appropriate or fit you situation. Note: both parties must initial all changes and modifications. This indicates that both parties (lessor and lessee) have agreed to the changes.

All things in life are negotiable, so be prepared to negotiate. To negotiate is defined as conferring with another or others in order to come to terms or reach an agreement. Some people find this process stressful while others thoroughly enjoy it. I suggest that you enjoy it as much as possible.

The following are basic rules or guidelines for successful negotiating:

a)   Be prepared. Understand your subject thoroughly. Be familiar with and passionate about what you want. The fact that you are reading this book will contribute greatly to your knowledge, and knowledge is power. Read and become familiar with the definitions in this book,

b)   Relax. Understand that this is only one deal and if you can't come to an agreement the world will not end. No matter how bad you want the house, don't settle for a deal that is bad for you or doesn't give you what you want; home ownership,

c)   Be reasonable. Be willing to give and take, but don't be a push over. If you are making an honest legitimate offer, the owner can't lose so don't be intimidated, and finally,

d)   Don't take the negotiations personally. This is a business deal. Some owners will be unreasonable and rude. They may want you to fail or at least make you feel bad. Don't let them move you from your goal and don't do business with people you don't like. You don't have to love them or want to be their buddies, but you at least need to feel comfortable around them and trust them. Avoid negative people. They will cause you grief.

The Addendum

The most critical part of the lease option is the addendum. This is where you will spell out the terms and condition of the option. The option will give you the opportunity to purchase the house at an agreed upon price within a pre-determined period of time, which usually is the same term as the lease. It should also describe any owner financing terms including down payment, interest rate, number of payments, amount and/or percentage of lease payment applied to down payment and amortization schedules. The addendum will be added to the lease and become part of it.

Attorneys and Realtors

I strongly recommend that prior to entering into a real estate contract or before signing any documents or depositing any earnest money; you consult with an attorney to ensure that your rights are properly protected. The owner will probably do the same thing.

A word of caution: sometimes an attorney can actually obstruct the process. I have had personal experiences where lawyers tried to either talk me or the seller out of the deal we had negotiated. If they had been able to do that, both of us would have lost. Of course the lawyer would still receive his fee. Just remember, nobody will care as much about your business and your future as you do. Do what is necessary and prudent to protect yourself, but do no not depend on anybody but yourself for the final decision.

The same is true for real estate agents. They make their living on commissions received from the sale property. This commission will automatically add from six to ten percent to the deal. This is cash that the owner has to pay when the house is sold. This will most likely increase your cash requirements. Also, most agents are not willing to wait a year or two to receive their commissions. I have negotiated deals through agents, but good ones who understand this process and who are willing to wait for their commissions are rare. In one case, I used the same agent to purchase a property and sell the same property. Because she was patient and professional, she made two commissions on the same house. Of course they were about six years apart, but income is income. Almost universally, agents and brokers work for the seller, not the buyer. They have a vested interest in promoting the seller's interest, not the buyer's.

Attorneys will charge you about $125+ per hour to counsel with you and review your documents. The best way to find a good attorney is by reference. Ask someone you know and trust to refer you to his or her lawyer. If this route is not available to you, search the Internet for "Attorneys - Referral Service". They can refer you to someone that is qualified to review your situation.

Let's review some of the things we've learned:

1.   The lease option terms are spelled out in writing in the addendum. An addendum is something added to the lease.

2.   The most critical part of the lease option is the addendum.

3.   Be an effective negotiator. Study your subject in order to know what you want. Don't be intimidated.

4.   The keys to effective negotiating are:
        a) Be prepared,
        b) Relax, and
        c) Be reasonable.

5.   It is recommended that you use an attorney to review documents before you sign them to protect your rights.

6.   Real estate agents work on commission almost exclusively for the seller.

CHAPTER 4
HOW MUCH CAN YOU AFFORD?

First of all, don't think you have to be a math wizard to understand home financing. Like most "esoteric" endeavors, professionals have created a cryptic language for dealing with mortgages. Use the glossary at the back of this book if you don't understand some specific term. Also, don't be afraid to ask, what does this mean? In my opinion, there are no dumb questions, only dumb answers.

If you were applying for a conventional loan, the lending agent (bank or Mortgage Company) would have very specific guidelines defining how much you could afford to pay each month for mortgage payments. These amounts would be based on your income and expenses. The formulas used to arrive at these numbers are called "qualifying ratios" because they are used to qualify or approve you for the loan. Basically, these are good guidelines for you to follow.

The "rule of thumb" to determine how much mortgage payment you can "afford" is an amount equal to a maximum of 28% of your gross monthly income.

As an example, if your combined annual net income is $96,000, your monthly income is that amount divided by twelve or $8,000 (only consider income that you can rely on). If you multiply that figure by 28%, you should be able to qualify for a monthly mortgage payment of about $1,100 per month. These amounts include principal, interest, taxes and insurance (PTTI).

Another ratio considered is your current debt. If you take your long-term expenses that extend more than eleven (11) months into the future (such as car loan payments) and add them to the projected mortgage payments (based on the above formula), your total should be a maximum of thirty six percent (36%) of your gross monthly income. Using the above example then, this figure should be about $1,440 per month. At the most, you are "qualified" if your long-term expenses don't exceed (based on the above formulas) a mortgage of $1,100 per month and long-term debt payments of $340 per month.

In addition, you should consider costs for utilities, insurance, and maintenance. The owner can give you the amount these costs have been in the past so that you can plan accordingly.

These guidelines have been developed over time to give the lender the greatest protection. They are, however, just guidelines. What you can afford is up to you. The best path for success is to plan and budget.

You should create a budget worksheet that lists your total income and your total expenses to determine what you can afford to spend on your house. With owner financing, there will be little restriction on the amount you pay. You don't have to "qualifier" based on the formulas used for conventional financing, as outlined in the above paragraph. You must, in a sense, qualify yourself. It is very important that you observe the following rules:

a)   Determine how much you can afford to pay,

b)   Make all payments as negotiated on time, and,

c)   Never "over extend" yourself financially.

Trite but true, "people don't plan to fail, they fail to plan" A little bit of planning and budgeting goes a long way. Use the budget worksheets located in the appendix as the basis for your planning.

Credit

Even if your income qualifies, you are not going to get a conventional loan unless you have either perfect or near perfect credit because credit is the next big qualifier. Being late, even on the smallest bill reflects negatively on your credit report. Some lenders are more lenient than others are, but all of them have tight credit requirements. I have never had my credit checked or even questioned when initiating a lease option/owner financing agreement. Most sellers either don't have the ability to get a credit report or don't care since they maintain ownership through the agreement, which gives them maximum protection in case of default.

If credit becomes an issue and the seller wants to know your history, be honest. You have nothing to gain from dishonesty. This agreement will be based in large part on trust, so honesty is required. Credit is secondary. Your ability to pay and your history of payments are primary.

If you want to get a copy of your credit report so that you are familiar with what's being reported, you can contact the three major credit bureaus directly. I have included addresses, phone numbers and web page information in the appendix.

To get a copy of your credit report contact the following credit agencies:
*   Equifax, 800-685-1111
*   Experian (formerly TRW), (888) EXPERIAN (397-3742)
*   Trans Union, 800-916-8800

As of the printing of this book, according to CNN, only Equifax offers consumers their FICO® or credit scores. These scores are used by lending intuitions to make decision about your credit worthiness. The following is an excerpt from the Equifax Credit Web Page, and I quote:
*   Your credit file can change - and change your credit score.
*   Your credit file and score are used to make decisions about loans, interest rates, even employment.
*   If your credit score drops - you can find out why and how to improve it.
*   Inaccurate information can hurt your credit score - you can verify the accuracy of your file.
*   Activity in your file, which you did not initiate, can be an early warning sign of identity theft.

Your FICO® Score

Equifax demystified credit scores by being the first credit-reporting agency to provide consumers access to their FICO credit score - the credit score used by the vast majority of lenders to determine a consumer's credit rating.

The FICO score, developed by Fair, Isaac (the pioneer in credit scoring) is a number between 300 and 850 that lenders use to determine your credit rating. A FICO score is a snapshot of your credit rating at a particular point in time. The higher your credit score the more likely you are to be approved for loans and receive favorable rates.

More than 70% of the 100 largest financial institutions use FICO scores to make billions of credit decisions each year, including more than 75 percent of mortgage loan originations.

Score Power™, from Equifax and Fair, Isaac, is the only online service that provides you access to your FICO credit score - the score most widely used in lending. In addition to your credit score, you receive the Equifax Credit Profile ® the score is based upon, a personalized analysis of your credit score, graphs showing how you rank among other consumers and tips on how to improve your credit rating.

Your personalized Score Power™ analysis will tell you who factors in your credit profile most affect your credit score and therefore your credit rating. The five areas considered in the calculation of your credit score listed from most important to least important are:

- Payment history
- Amount owed
- Length of credit history
- New credit
- Types of credit in use

Check out Score Power™ to learn your FICO® credit score - and how to improve and manage your overall credit health.
Experian's Web address is: www.experian.com/consumer/

I highly recommend you get a copy of your current credit report so that you will have a good idea of where you stand. However, lease option/owner financing is perfect for those who have the financial resources, but don't have the credit. It is particularly ideal for self-employed or first time buyers. It allows you to enjoy all the benefits associated with the conventional loan with much less hassle, headache and expense.

Again, let's review:

1.   Rule of thumb qualifying numbers - 28% of total income, 36% of total expense should be spent on your mortgage and long-term debt.

2.   However, you will qualify yourself through your demeanor and trustworthiness.

3.   Create and use a budget worksheet to determine how much you can afford.

4.   With lease options and owner financing, credit is secondary; ability to pay and payment history are primary.

CHAPTER 5
OWNER FINANCING

Owner financing is a legal, legitimate way for people to buy and sell property. It provides an opportunity for you, whether the buyer or seller, to finance property. It is especially appropriate if you cannot qualify for conventional financing. Even if you can get a loan from a lender, owner financing can sometimes be a better deal. It can be infinitely less complicated and much cheaper. Plus you can negotiate more flexible and applicable terms such as length of mortgage, interest rates, down payments, etc.

Although I have recommended throughout this book that you use the lease option/owner financing method, you can acquire owner financing without leasing the property first. I recommend a lease/option on the purchase of your primary residence for the following reasons:

a)   It affords you an opportunity to live with the property for at least a year before you buy,

b)   You can accrue (build) and save your down payment and,

c)   It gives you a "payment history" and builds trust levels with the seller/financier.

If the above conditions are not applicable to your situation, then you can shop for houses that advertise as "for sale by owner", "terms available" or "owner financing available" Regardless, the information that follows will apply to either strategy. Direct owner financing is more appropriate for non-owner occupied properties such as raw land, investment, commercial and vacation properties.

Owner financing is available and can be negotiated on single-family homes, condominiums, duplexes, apartments, investment property, raw land, vacation homes and commercial property. Since the real estate itself provides the collateral for the financing, the owner is protected. Real estate is the best and safest collateral you can have.

How to Establish Current Value of the Property

The simplest and most effective way to establish a value for the property you are considering leasing and/or purchasing is to acquire an appraisal from a licensed appraiser. This usually cost around $600-1,200 dollars but can save you a considerable amount of distress later on. In order to establish a lease option agreement, the buyer and the seller need to agree upon a price or value for the property.

Appraisers can be found with an Internet search for Real Estate – Appraisers. Try to find someone that is located in the community and/or neighborhood where the property is located. They are sometimes more aware of the market values for that particular area. Use the appraisal to protect yourself from paying an inflated price.

If the appraised price and the price that the owner is asking are very close, then you are probably okay. Some owners will ask an inflated price in order to cover for appreciation over time. I would not recommend that you pay more than five percent over appraised value. If the owner is asking the appraised value and/or less, then you are probably safe.

There is an alternative method to using an appraiser. It requires that you access the database at your county tax assessor's office. This information is public record. You can look up similar houses or properties in the same neighborhood that have sold over the past year. The average of these sales should give you an idea of what the property is worth. Contact your local county assessor's office and inquire as to procedure. There is usually no cost except for copies.

Balloon Payments

Most owner financing contains a balloon payment. There has been a lot of negative talk about balloon payments in the last few years, but once you understand and plan for them, they can be a valuable and necessary tool. A balloon payment is defined as a final payment on a loan that pays the loan balance in full.

A common practice in owner financing is to amortize the mortgage, that is develop a payment plan, based on twenty to thirty year financing but with the balance due in full after five to ten years. This final payment is a balloon payment and pays off the loan. The reason this is done is to lower your monthly payments and at the same time, shorten the length of time an owner has to carry the agreement.

For example, you negotiate a mortgage on a $100,000 house. After paying $5,000 down, the balance of $95,000 is amortized at 9% interest over ten years. This would create a payment of $1,140 per month. This same deal amortized over twenty years would give you a payment of $855 per month or a difference of $285 per month for ten years. Your final payment, with the twenty-year amortization, would be $67,000 after ten years. If you can structure the deal without a balloon payment, do so. If monthly cash flow is important, customize the amortization to fit your particular circumstances.

With a balloon payment, you will need to get a new loan, most likely conventional, after ten years. Usually this isn't a problem because, with minimal appreciation, you will have an excellent equity position in your home. Appreciation is defined as a rise in value or price over time. If the $100,000 property appreciates at 5% per year, its value at the end of ten years would be $ 164,000. Therefore, your equity would be $96,000. You would need a loan equal to 41% of the value of your property. You can usually get a non-qualifying conventional loan at this level. The Seller's Incentive

What's the incentive for the seller? Actually, it's quite simple. First, there is a much greater return on their investment if they are willing to finance the sale and willing to take their income over an extended period of time. For example, a house being sold for $100,000 cash will bring the owner his equity in cash less his sales expense. These expenses include real estate commissions, escrow fees, attorney's fees, etc. If he has a mortgage of $85,000 on the house, the gross equity is $15,000. After expenses, which can run ten percent (10%) or higher, the net is only $5,000 or about 5%, period. See Figure 4 below.

Return on Property Sold the "Conventional" Way:

Sales Price of House	$100,000
Less Mortgage Balance	$ 85,000
Gross Equity	$ 15,000
Less Sales Cost	$ 10,000
Net to Seller	$ 5,000

In addition, there is a capital gains tax of 28% to consider which could reduce the seller's net income even more.

If they sell and finance that same house for $100,000 either as a lease option/owner finance or direct owner finance, look how the profit picture changes:

First, they can finance the house with up to a ten- percent down payment and an interest rate in the range of 9% amortized for a term of twenty years. The seller will receive $184,000 for the same house or a difference of nearly $80,000.

Second, it is a very secure investment for the seller. The house itself is the collateral. If for some reason you default on the contract, even after nine years (very unlikely) they would retain ownership of the house plus all the money you have paid plus any equity that has accrued.

Lease Option/Owner Financing (Example) - The Seller's Incentive

Activity	Explanation	Dollar Amount
Lease Payments	1 Year @ $800 per Month	$9,600 per Year
Applied to Down Payment	20% of Lease Payments	$1,920 per Year
Down Payment @ 5%	$5,000 Less Applied Amount	$3,080 ($5,000-1,920)
Monthly Mortgage @ 9%	Amortized 20 years, due in 10	$855.00
Total Payments Received	Lease & Mortgage Payments +Down	$115,300
Balance Due in 10 Years	Balloon Payment - Cash to Seller	$67,800
Total Received from Property	All Payments =	$183,100
Value of House in 10 Years@ 5% Appreciation per Year =		$164,000
Net Sale for seller through Owner Financing		
Difference from Starting Balance on Property plus cash received		$98,100
Net From Conventional Sale	Sold for "CASH" @ $100,000	$5,000
Average Income Per Year	Total Payments divided by 10	$11,500 (plus balloon)
Equity (Security) in Property After 10 Years, Depending on Seller's Mortgage Balance = $100,000 (+/-)		

The Seller has a very secure income each month for ten years. Although income to the seller is subject to tax, interest payments on the first mortgage and any property tax are generally deductible.

The Buyers Incentive

I've already discussed some the advantages and benefits of home ownership such as pride of ownership, security, status, appreciation, equity and potential tax savings. With lease option and/or owner financing you can take advantage of all the above benefits. Additionally, the lack or reduction of qualifying requirements, red tape, closing costs, escrow fees and other related costs/requirements make the purchase of a home a reality for almost everyone.

Financially, the purchase of a home can be one of the best and most important investments you ever make. However, this is not a short-term investment. Most mortgages are amortized over twenty or thirty years. With owner financing, it is unlikely that the financing will be for more than ten years. People don't live as long as banks. However, as I describe above under balloon payments, you can base your payments on a longer period of time in order to make them affordable. The following projection uses the same scenario as the seller's incentive example above.

Activity	Explanation	Dollar Amount
Lease Payments	One Year @ $800 per Month	$9,600 per Year
Applied to Down Payment	20% of Lease Payment	$1,920
Down Payment @ 5%	$5,000 Less Applied Amount	$3,080 ($5,000-1,920)
Balance to Financed	$100,000 Sales Prices Less Down	$95,000
Monthly Mortgage Payments-9%	Interest-Amortized 20 Years	$855.00
Total Interest Payments	Could be Deductible	$70,400
Total Payments	Principle & Interest - 10 Years	$102,600
Value of Property - 10 Years	@ 5% Appreciation per Year	$155,000
Balance Due - 10 Years	Balloon Payment (New Loan, Cash)	$ 67,800
Buyer's Equity - 10 Years	Value Less Balance Due	$ 87,000
Per Cent New Loan to Value - Per Cent of Value Needed for Balloon Payment - 44%		

Real estate Interest payments are deductible on your income tax, as is real estate taxes. The buyer could deduct up to $70,000 in interest payments over 10 years.

Appreciation
Appreciation is defined as a rise in value over time. Houses appreciate at different rates depending on various factors. Some of these factors are location, condition, configuration and the housing market. How much a house appreciates will differ from neighborhood to neighborhood, but generally, good houses in good neighborhoods have a decent appreciation rate.

To predict the appreciation of a property over time, take the beginning value of the property. In the sample chart below, this value is $100,000. If this property appreciates at an average rate of 5% per year, it would be worth $115,763 after four years and $155,133 after the tenth year. Appreciation is cumulative, that is, each year's appreciation is based on the previous year's appreciated value.

To project future cumulative appreciation, use the chart below. Select the historic appreciation percentage and multiply the current value times the factor listed on the chart. Using the example above, the current value of the house is $100, 000. The average appreciation over the past 10 years has been 5.0 percent. Using this as a basis for projection, multiply $100,000 times 1.55 (the factor given for 5 percent appreciation per year over 10 years) and that will give you the projected value of the home in 10 years with an average 5% appreciation per year. In this case, the house would be worth $155,000 by the 10th year. Equity in the house would be $155,000 minus the principal amount owed (this usually is the same as your balloon payment).

Keep in mind that many factors impact appreciation rates and houses can either appreciate faster are slower than they have historically. This chart simply gives you a basis to projects value of the house based on average historical appreciation. What you may experience could be significantly different.

Appreciation Rates Over Ten Years

Percent Appreciation per Year
Factor

1 %	1.09
2 %	1.20
3 %	1.31
4 %	1.42
5 %	1.55

The bottom line is as follows: your incentive, under the above scenario, is $87,000 in equity and a possible $70,000 in income tax deductions over ten years. Remember, these are only examples, your situation will be different depending on sales price, interest rates, terms, down payment, tax rates, etc., but the fundamentals are the same. I have included blank worksheets in the appendix for your use.

Down Payment
The amount of cash you apply against the sales price of the house is considered your down payment. If you are leasing with option, you will know a year to two in advance how much you will need to close the deal on the house. This gives you an opportunity to acquire the cash needed to purchase the house. It will take planning, budgeting and some sacrifice, but the rewards of home ownership are worth it. Normally, a down payment will range between 5% and 20% of the purchase price. However, this figure is subject to negotiation, so don't get discouraged. I have paid between nothing and ten percent down.

The amount you negotiate for a down payment will depend on your circumstances. If you have access to cash from savings, retirement, insurance, the sale of property, etc., a larger down payment will give you more equity and lower monthly payments. If you are relatively cash poor, you will want to negotiate a smaller down payment.

Only commit to a down payment with which you feel comfortable. Don't set yourself up with an amount you cannot possible manage.

As example, the difference between monthly mortgage payments on a $100,000 mortgage financed at 9% interest, amortized over twenty years due in ten, is $45 per month more if you put a 5% ($5,000) down payment versus a 10% ($10,000) down payment. This extra payment lasts, in this example, for ten years (120 months). That's a total cost to you of $5,400 in extra payments over ten years. Less your additional $5,000 down payment, this equals an extra cost of $400. The net cost to you, therefore, is $3.34 per month. You decide if it's worth it or not.

Every dollar you pay down, however, is a dollar more in equity. So the decision should be based on what you can afford both to put down and to pay per month. Again, you should negotiate based on your specific circumstances.

I used the equity from my first house as down payment on my second house. However, I leased with option for a year, even though I had the down payment, with part of my lease payment going against my down payment. This allowed me to get interest on my savings, reduced my down payment requirements and I gained a year of appreciation since I fixed the price with the option.

Interest

The interest rate you pay will be negotiated between you and the seller. Usually, if the seller has a mortgage on the property, he will want a percentage point or two above what he is currently paying. Because the seller is providing the financing, you may pay a different interest rate (higher or lower) than what is available from a conventional lender. Normally, the interest rate will be based on what is currently available in the market. You can call local lenders (banks, mortgage companies, etc.) and ask what their current interest rates are. This will give you some basis for negotiation.

To give you an idea of the impact of the interest rate on monthly mortgage payments, review the following table:

Monthly Payment per $1,000 Financed by Seller

Interest Rate	10 Years	15 Years	20 Years	30 Years
7.0 %	$11.61	$ 8.99	$ 7.75	$ 6.65
7.5 %	$ 11.87	$ 9.26	$ 8.06	$ 6.99
8.0 %	$ 12.13	$ 9.56	$ 8.36	$ 7.34
8.5 %	$ 12.40	$ 9.85	$ 8.68	$ 7.69
9.0 %	$ 12.67	$ 10.14	$ 9.00	$ 8.05

To use the table above, divide the mortgage amount by one thousand, and then multiply by the payment amount. For example, a mortgage of $95,000, amortized over twenty years at 9.0% would have a monthly payment of $810.00. To get the monthly payment, use the following formula: $95,000 divided by 1,000 = 95 X $9.00 = $855.00 per month. Use this information to determine the monthly payment required for the property you are considering.

Terms

Terms can be defined as the elements of a proposed or concluded agreement or the conditions of an agreement. The terms of the agreement include interest rate, amortization schedules, monthly payments inclusive of tax and insurance payments, late fees, payment dates, default procedures and generally the requirements that the buyer and the seller must meet in order to satisfy the negotiated agreement. The terms should be fair and protective to both the buyer and the seller. Please see the sample Agreement for Deed for suggested term descriptions.

Recording the Deed

The agreement for deed should be recorded with the County Recording Office. The procedure for doing this varies by locale, but in general, the following requirements will serve as a general guideline:

Deed Requirements
(See Sample Deed in Sample Documents Section)
1. Grantors (Party Giving Title) names legibly printed in the body of the Deed
2. Grantors' mailing address
3. Grantees (Party Receiving Title) names legibly printed in the body of the Deed
4. Grantees' mailing address
5. Legal description of property
6. Signatures of grantors
7. Names printed under their signature
8. Names of witnesses printed under their signatures
9. Complete notary acknowledgment:
a) Names being acknowledged
b) Date acknowledgment taken
c) Signature of notary
d) Name printed under signature
e) Commission expiration date
f) Seal
10. "Prepared by" statement (name and address of the person preparing the Deed)

Note: These are recording requirements for Deeds. There are other statutory requirements for making a conveyance valid, which are not within the scope of the recording office to dictate.

Normally, it takes four to six business days to record a deed received by mail. However, in times of extremely heavy volume, it is possible that there may be delays up to twenty business days. If time is of the essence, you should consider taking the document into the office and waiting for it to be recorded.

If you are recording your document by mail and want the original document returned, you should enclose a self-addressed stamped envelope. Make certain that adequate postage for the weight of the document is affixed to the envelope.

Legal advice cannot be provided.

County records staff cannot help you complete deed forms or give legal advice of any type. If you have questions about completing forms or the proper method of transferring property, you should consult an attorney.
The following are examples of typical recording fees. Of course these fees will vary by county:

$6.00 for the first page, $4.50 for each additional page - If a page is typed or printed on both front and back, it will be considered two pages.
A Documentary Stamp Fee of $0.70 per each $100.00 or fraction thereof on the purchase price of the property. If there is NO money involved in the sale, there is a minimum fee of $0.70

Copy Fee $1.00 per page Closing and Costs - Closing costs are those expenses, paid by both the seller and buyer, associated with the sale and financing of the property. These costs can be negotiated between the buyer and seller as to who will pay. With a conventional loan, these cost can run between three and six percent (3% - 6%) of the mortgage amount. Usually, with seller financing, these costs will be minimal.

Title Insurance

The buyer will also pay for any title insurance premiums. A title insurance company usually issues title insurance. The purpose of this policy is to protect the buyer from any errors that show up in a title search. The premium is normally based on the value of the property.

When you exercise your lease option and/or use owner financing to buy your home or property, you don't receive the land itself, but a title to the property. This title may be limited by rights and/or claims asserted by others. Problems with title can reduce your use and enjoyment of the property as well as be a potential financial loss.

Unlike other types of insurance that are paid an annual basis and concentrate on future loss, title insurance is a onetime premium paid at the time you purchase the property. It is designed to be a safeguard against a "defective" property title. These "defects" can be things like existing deeds that contain improper names, judgments, tax liens, easements and outstanding mortgages.

Owner's title insurance is normally issued in the amount of the real estate purchase and exists as long as the insured has a vested interest in the property.

Title insurance begins with the search of public land records. The intent of this search is to identify any matters that may have a negative effect on the issuance of a clear title. Many times, if there are issues, they are found in the history of ownership of the property. These items would need to be corrected in order for a clear title to be conveyed.

Even with a title search, there are certain items that could remain hidden and would emerge only after completion of the purchase. These issues can be a costly surprise. Examples of these types of issues are; mistakes in public records, forged documents, and/or undisclosed claims against the property. Title insurance, theoretically, can protect the buyer against claims and loss generated by such hidden issues.

A list of companies that sell title insurance can be found with an Internet search of "Insurance - Title". In addition, I have listed the address and phone number of the American Land Title Association in the index. They should be able to help you find an appropriate agent.

Other Expenses

If the seller has engaged a Realtor to sell or lease his property, he will be responsible for paying any commissions due upon execution of the deal.
Other costs traditionally paid by the buyer are as follows: home inspection (if necessary), and recording the deed. You will also pay for your lawyer's fees to review any documents.

Chapter Five in Review

1.   Owner financing is a legitimate way for people to buy and sell property of all kinds including single-family homes, duplexes, apartments, condominiums, investment   property, raw land, vacation homes and commercial property.

2.   Most owner financing includes balloon payments. A balloon payment is a final   payment that pays the balance of the loan in full.

3.   A balloon payment allows the buyer to have lower monthly payments.

4.   If the seller provides financing he can have a very safe investment that has excellent return over time.

5.   The buyer will have gain ownership, tax deductions and equity at the end of the financing period.

6.   Houses appreciate or increase in value over time.

7.   Down payments are negotiable and can run from between five and ten percent.

8.   Interest is negotiable and is usually based on the seller's first mortgage or the   prevailing interest rates.

9.   Terms of the financing include amortization schedules, monthly mortgage payments, late fees and policy, insurance, taxes, and general requirements of the agreement.

10.   The deed should be recorded with your county records division.

CHAPTER 6
EQUAL OPPORTUNITY HOUSING

The Fair Housing Act of 1968

All real estate sold in the United States is subject to the US Federal Fair Housing Act of 1968, as amended. This Act makes it illegal to advertise or sell property based on "any preference, limitation or discrimination based on race, color, religion, sex, handicap, family status or national origin or an intention to make any such preference, limitation or discrimination." State and local laws may add additional prohibitions against discrimination based on age, parental status, sexual orientation, political ideology, and financial status. The preceding list is by no means meant to be all-inclusive. If you have questions or think you have been the subject of discrimination, check with you local housing authority or the US Department of Housing and Urban Development (HUD). You can call HUD toll free at 1-800-347-3735.

CHAPTER 7
A FINAL WORD

"If l were asked to name the chief benefit of the house, I should say: the house shelters daydreaming, the house protects the dreamer, the house allows one to dream in peace." Gaston Bachelard (1884-1962), French philosopher.

After twenty years and numerous "agreements", I can say with confidence that this is a little promoted and used opportunity.   Many sellers are scared to get involved with this kind of mortgage because they have been "burned" before or they have heard all the horror stories about other people who have. Don't let that stop or discourage you. The fact is that this technique is a genuine "win - win" situation for both the buyer and the seller. The seller will significantly increase the income from the sale of their home and the buyer will be given an opportunity to own their home and enjoy the benefits of home ownership. The best advice I can give you is, don't be discouraged and don't lose focus. You now have in your hands a system that can create the opportunity for you to fulfill the dream of owning your own home or property.

Over the years, I have fielded hundreds of questions from friends and family, wanting to know how I was able to buy beautiful homes with such favorable terms. They were all fascinated by the concepts that I shared with them. I have also had some very positive experiences in working directly with the sellers. But let's be honest, I have also learned and developed this system the hard way, through trial and error. By following my system and benefiting from my experience, you can avoid those pitfalls.

Buying a home or property with a lease option/owner financing strategy will require that the parties involved trust one another. Let's face it; it all boils down to the fundamental agreement between two people.

One of the main reasons I wrote this book was to share with others the opportunities I have had. I have personally known the joy and benefit of home and property ownership. I want you to have that same experience. Go for it and Good Luck!

The Author
J. Mark Eason

CHAPTER 8
DEFINITIONS

The prospective homebuyer will find this terminology helpful for understanding words and terms used in real estate transactions. There are, however, some factors that may affect these definitions:

• Terms are defined as they are commonly understood in the mortgage and real estate industry. The same terms may have different meanings in another context.
• The definitions are intentionally general, non-technical and short. They do not encompass all possible meanings or nuances that a term may acquire in legal use.
• State laws, as well as custom and use in various States or regions of the country, may modify or completely change the meanings of certain terms defined.
• Terms are defined as they are commonly understood in the mortgage and real estate industry. The same terms may have different meanings in another context.
• The definitions are intentionally general, non-technical and short. They do not encompass all possible meanings or nuances that a term may acquire in legal use.
• State laws, as well as custom and use in various States or regions of the country, may modify or completely change the meanings of certain terms defined.

-A-

Abstract (Of Title)
A summary of the public records relating to the title to a particular piece of land.

Acceleration Clause
Condition in a mortgage that may require the balance of the loan to become due immediately, if regular mortgage payments are not made or for breach of other conditions of the mortgage.

Agreement for Deed
Known by various names, such as agreement for sale, contract of purchase, purchase agreement, or sales agreement according to location or jurisdiction. A contract in which a seller agrees to sell and a buyer agrees to buy, under certain specific terms and conditions spelled out in writing and signed by both parties.

Amortization
A payment plan, which enables the borrower to reduce his debt gradually through monthly payments of principal.

Appurtenance
A right, privilege, or property that is considered necessary to the principal property for purposes such as passage of title, conveyance, or inheritance.

Appraisal
An expert judgment or estimate of the quality or value of real estate as of a given date.

Appreciation
A rise in value or price, especially over time.

Assumption of Mortgage
An obligation undertaken by the purchaser of property to be personally liable for payment of an existing mortgage. In an assumption, the purchaser is substituted for the original mortgagor in the mortgage instrument and the original mortgagor is to be released from further liability in the assumption, the mortgagee's consent is usually required. The original mortgagor should always obtain a written release from further liability if he desires to be fully released under the assumption. Failure to obtain such a release renders the original mortgagor liable if the person assuming the mortgage fails to make the monthly payments.
An "Assumption of Mortgage" is often confused with "purchasing subject to a mortgage." When one purchases subject to a mortgage, the purchaser agrees to make the monthly mortgage payments on an existing mortgage, but the original mortgagor remains personally liable if the purchaser fails to make the monthly payments. Since the original mortgagor remains liable in the event of default, the mortgagee's consent is not required to a sale subject to a mortgage.
Both "Assumption of Mortgage" and "Purchasing Subject to a Mortgage" are used to finance the sale of property. They may also be used when a mortgagor is in financial difficulty and desires to sell the property to avoid foreclosure.

-B-

Binder or Offer to Purchase
A preliminary agreement, secured by the payment of earnest money, between a buyer and seller as an offer to purchase real estate. A binder secures the right to purchase real estate upon agreed terms for a limited period of time. If the buyer changes his mind or is unable to purchase, the earnest money is forfeited unless the binder expressly provides that it is to be refunded.

Balloon Payment
A final payment that pays the balance of a mortgage loan in full.

Broker
(See real estate broker)

-C-

Certificate of Title
A certificate issued by a title company or a written opinion rendered by an attorney that the seller has good marketable and insurable title to the property, which he is offering for sale. A certificate of title offers no protection against any hidden defects in the title, which an examination of the records could not reveal. The issuer of a certificate of title is liable only for damages due to negligence. The protection offered a homeowner under a certificate of title is not as great as that offered in a title insurance policy.

Closing Costs

The numerous expenses which buyers and sellers normally incur to complete a transaction in the transfer of ownership of real estate. These costs are in addition to price of the property and are items prepaid at the closing day. This is a typical list:

Buyer's Expense
Documentary Stamps on Notes
Recording Deed and Mortgage
Escrow Fees
Attorney's Fee
Title Insurance
Appraisal and Inspection
Survey Charges
Seller's Expense
Cost of Abstract
Real Estate Commission
Survey Charge
Escrow Fees
Recording Mortgage
Documentary Stamps on Deed
Attorney's Fees

The agreement of sale negotiated previously between the buyer and the seller should state, in writing, who will pay each of the above costs.

Cloud (On Title)
An outstanding claim or encumbrance which adversely affects the marketability of title.
Commission
Money paid to a real estate agent or broker by the seller as compensation for finding a buyer and completing the sale. Usually it is a percentage of the sale price, six to seven percent (6% - 7%) on houses, ten percent (10 %) on land.

Condominium
Individual ownership of a dwelling unit and an individual interest in the common areas and facilities that serve the multi-unit project.

Contract of Purchase
(See agreement of sale)

Conventional Mortgage
A mortgage loan not insured by HUD or guaranteed by the Veterans' Administration. It is subject to conditions established by the lending institution and State statutes. The mortgage rates may vary with different institutions and between States. (States have various interest limits.)

-D-

Deed
The deed is a formal written instrument by which title to real property is transferred from one owner to another. The deed should contain an accurate description of the property being conveyed, should be signed and witnessed according to the laws of the State where the property is located, and should be delivered to the purchaser at closing. There are two parties to a deed: the grantor and the grantee. (See also deed of trust, general warranty deed, quitclaim deed, and special warranty deed.)

Default
Failure to make mortgage payments as agreed to in a commitment based on the terms and at the designated time set forth in the mortgage or deed of trust. It is the mortgagor's responsibility to remember the due date and send the payment prior to the due date, not after. Generally, thirty days after the due date if payment is not received, the mortgage is in default. In the event of default, the mortgage may give the lender the right to accelerate payments, take possession and receive rents, and start foreclosure. Defaults may also come about by the failure to observe other conditions in the mortgage or agreement for deed.

Depreciation
Decline in value of a house due to wear and tear, adverse changes in the neighborhood, or any other reason.

Documentary Stamps
A State tax, in the forms of stamps, required on deeds and mortgages when real estate title passes from one owner to another. The amount of stamps required varies with each State.

Down payment
The amount of money to be paid by the purchaser to the seller upon the signing of the agreement of sale. The agreement of sale will refer to the down payment amount and will acknowledge receipt of the down payment. Down payment is the difference between the sales price and maximum mortgage amount. The down payment may not be refundable if the purchaser fails to buy the property without good cause. If the purchaser wants the down payment to be refundable, he should insert a clause in the agreement of sale specifying the conditions under which the deposit will be refunded, if the agreement does not already contain such clause. If the seller cannot deliver good title, the agreement of sale usually requires the seller to return the down payment and to pay interest and expenses incurred by the purchaser.

-E-

Earnest Money - The deposit money given to the seller or his agent by the potential buyer upon the signing of the agreement of sale to show that he is serious about buying the house. If the sale goes through, the earnest money is applied against the down payment. If the sale does not go through, the earnest money will be forfeited or lost unless the binder or offer to purchase expressly provides that it is refundable.

Encumbrance
A legal right or interest in land that affects a good or clear title, and diminishes the land's value. It can take numerous forms, such as zoning ordinances, easement rights, claims, mortgages, liens, charges, a pending legal action, unpaid taxes, or restrictive covenants. An encumbrance does not legally prevent transfer of the property to another. A title search is all that is usually done to reveal the existence of such encumbrances, and it is up to the buyer to determine whether he wants to purchase with the encumbrance, or what can be done to remove it.

Equity
The value of a homeowner's unencumbered interest in real estate. Equity is computed by subtracting from the property's fair market value the total of the unpaid mortgage balance and any outstanding liens or other debts against the property. A homeowner's equity increases as he pays off his mortgage or as the property appreciates in value. When the mortgage and all other debts against the property are paid in full the homeowner has 100% equity in his property.

Escrow
Funds paid by one party to another (the escrow agent) to hold until the occurrence of a specified event, after which the funds are released to a designated individual. In FHA mortgage transactions an escrow account usually refers to the funds a mortgagor pays the lender at the time of the periodic mortgage payments. The money is held in a trust fund, provided by the lender for the buyer. Such funds should be adequate to cover yearly-anticipated expenditures for mortgage insurance premiums, taxes, hazard insurance premiums, and special assessments.

-F-

Foreclosure
A legal term applied to any of the various methods of enforcing payment of the debt secured by a mortgage, or deed of trust, by taking and selling the mortgaged property, and depriving the mortgagor of possession.

-G-

General Warranty Deed
A deed which conveys not only all the grantor's interests in and title to the property to the grantee, but also warrants that if the title is defective or has a "cloud" on it (such as mortgage claims, tax liens, title claims, judgments, or mechanic's liens against it) the grantee may hold the grantor liable.

Grantee
That party in the deed who is the buyer or recipient.

Grantor
That party in the deed who is the seller or giver.

-H-

Hazard Insurance
Protects against damages caused to property by fire, windstorms, and other common hazards.

Hereditaments
Property that can be inherited.

HUD
US Department of Housing and Urban Development. Office of Housing/Federal Housing Administration within HUD insures home mortgage loans made by lenders and sets minimum standards for such homes.

-I-

Interest
A charge paid for borrowing money. (See mortgage note)

-L-

Lien
A claim by one person on the property of another as security for money owed. Such claims may include obligations not met or satisfied, judgments, unpaid taxes, materials, or labor. (See also special lien.)

-M-

Marketable Title
A title that is free and clear of objectionable liens, clouds, or other title defects. A title which enables an owner to sell his property freely to others and which others will accept without objection.

Mortgage
A lien or claim against real property given by the buyer to the lender as security for money borrowed. Under government-insured or loan-guarantee provisions, the payments may include escrow amounts covering taxes, hazard insurance, water charges, and special assessments. Mortgages generally run from 10 to 30 years, during which the loan is to be paid off.

Mortgage Commitment
A written notice from the bank or other lending institution saying it will advance mortgage funds in a specified amount to enable a buyer to purchase a house.

Mortgage Note
A written agreement to repay a loan. The agreement is secured by a mortgage, serves as proof of indebtedness, and states the manner in which it shall be paid. The note states the actual amount of the debt that the mortgage secures and renders the mortgagor personally responsible for repayment.

Mortgage (open-end)
A mortgage with a provision that permits borrowing additional money in the future without refinancing the loan or paying additional financing charges. Open-end provisions often limit such borrowing to no more than would raise the balance to the original loan figure.

Mortgagee
The lender in a mortgage agreement.

Mortgagor
The borrower in a mortgage agreement.

-P-

Points
Sometimes called "discount points." A point is one percent of the amount of the mortgage loan. For example, if a loan is for $100,000, one point is $1,000. Points are charged by a lender to raise the yield on his loan at a time when money is tight, interest rates are high, and there is a legal limit to the interest rate that can be charged on a mortgage. Buyers are prohibited from paying points on HLJD or Veterans' Administration guaranteed loans (sellers can pay, however). On a conventional mortgage points may be paid by either buyer or seller or split between them.

Prepayment
Payment of mortgage loan, or part of it, before due date. Mortgage agreements often restrict the right of prepayment either by limiting the amount that can be prepaid in any one year or charging a penalty for prepayment.

Principal
The basic element of the loan as distinguished from interest and mortgage insurance premium. In other words, principal is the amount upon which interest is paid.

Purchase Agreement
See agreement of sale.

-Q-

Quitclaim Deed
A deed which transfers whatever interest the maker of the deed may have in the particular parcel of land. A quitclaim deed is often given to clear the title when the grantor's interest in a property is questionable. By accepting such a deed the buyer assumes all the risks. Such a deed makes no warranties as to the title, but simply transfers to the buyer whatever interest the grantor has. (See deed.)

-R-

Real Estate Broker
A middleman or agent who buys and sells real estate for a company, firm, or individual on a commission basis. The broker does not have title to the property, but generally represents the owner.

Refinancing
The process of the same mortgagor paying off one loan with the proceeds from another loan.

Restrictive Covenants
Private restrictions limiting the use of real property. Restrictive covenants are created by deed and may "run with the land," binding all subsequent purchasers of the land, or may be "personal" and binding only between the original seller and buyer.

-S-

Sales Agreement
See agreement of sale.

Special Assessments
A special tax imposed on property, individual lots or all property in the immediate area, for road construction, sidewalks, sewers, streetlights, etc.

Special Lien
A lien that binds a specified piece of property, unlike a general lien, which is levied against all one's assets. It creates a right to retain something of value belonging to another person as compensation for labor, material, or money expended in that person's behalf. In some localities it is called "particular" lien or "specific" lien. (See lien.)

Special Warranty Deed
A deed in which the grantor conveys title to the grantee and agrees to protect the grantee against title defects or claims asserted by the grantor and those persons whose right to assert a claim against the title arose during the period the grantor held title to the property. In a special warranty deed the grantor guarantees to the grantee that he has done nothing during the time he held title to the property which has, or which might in the future, impair the grantee's title.

State Stamps
See documentary stamps

Survey
A map or plat made by a licensed surveyor showing the results of measuring the land with its elevations, improvements, boundaries, and its relationship to surrounding tracts of land. A survey is often required by the lender to assure him that a building is actually sited on the land according to its legal description.

-T-
Tax
As applied to real estate, an enforced charge imposed on persons, property or income, to be used to support the State. The governing body in turn utilizes the funds in the best interest of the general public.

Title
As generally used, the rights of ownership and possession of particular property. In real estate usage, title may refer to the instruments or documents by which a right of ownership is established (title documents), or it may refer to the ownership interest one has in the real estate.

Title Insurance
Protects lenders or homeowners against loss of their interest in property due to legal defects in title. Title insurance may be issued to a "mortgagee's title policy." Insurance benefits will be paid only to the "named insured" in the title policy, so it is important that an owner purchase an "owner's title policy", if he desires the protection of title insurance.

Title Search
A check of the title records, generally at the local courthouse, to make sure the buyer is purchasing a house from the legal owner and there are no liens, overdue special assessments, or other claims or outstanding restrictive covenants filed in the record, which would adversely affect the marketability or value of title.

-Z-

Zoning Ordinances
Zoning ordinances are the acts of an authorized local government establishing building codes, and setting forth regulations for property land usage.

APPENDIX

Budget Worksheet

Use this worksheet to determine your financial position. It will also help you decide how much you can afford to pay for monthly mortgage payments.

Income - Monthly
Husband Salary _____ (Net, after Taxes)
Wife Salary _____ (Net, after Taxes)
Other Income _____ (Net, after Taxes)
Total Monthly Income _____ (Add all of the Above)
Fixed Expenses - Monthly
Projected "Affordable" Mortgage Payment
Total Monthly Income x .28 = _____
(Principal, Interest, Taxes and Insurance)
Auto (Payments) _____
Installment Loans _____ (Department Stores, etc.)
Sub-Total _____ (Total Long Term Liabilities)
Projected Total Affordable Expenses
Total Long Term Liabilities x .36 = _____

Variable expenses - Monthly

Automobile _____ (Gasoline, Maintenance)
Child Care _____ (Day Care, Pre-School, etc.)
Clothes _____ (New, cleaners, etc.)
Credit Cards _____ (Monthly Payments)
Food _____ (Groceries, etc.)
Insurance _____ (Auto, Health, Life, etc.)
Medical _____ (Doctor Visits, Prescriptions)
Miscellaneous _____ (All other expenses)
Phone _____
School _____ (Supplies, Tuition, Books, etc.)
Utilities _____ (Electric, Gas, Cable)

Sub-Total _____ (Variable Expense)

Total Monthly Expenses_____
(Short Term [Variable] and Long Term [Fixed] Expenses)

Total Net _____(Total Income Minus Total Expenses)
This is the money (net) available for savings, down payment, emergencies and miscellaneous spending.

Worksheets

Use the following worksheets to figure the lease option/owner financing strategy on any particular house. Please review the information contained in Chapter 5 to assist in completing the following worksheets:

Sales Price of Home or Property

$

Budget Information (From Budget Worksheet)	**Monthly**	**Annually**
Net Income	$	$
Amount Available for Mortgage Payments	$	$

Lease Option	Monthly	Annually
Amount of Payment	$	$
Applied to Down (Amount or Percent)	$	$
Length in Time (Months or Years)	$	$
Deposit	$	$

Owner Financing

Mortgage Balance (after down payment)	Amount	$
Interest Rate	Amount	%
Amortization (Number of years used to figure Mortgage Payment)	Years	
Monthly Mortgage Payment	Amount	$
Balloon Payment Amount	Amount	$
Total Interest Paid	Amount	$
Projected Value of House or Property at End of Term	Amount	$
Projected Equity at End of Term	Amount	$

SAMPLE FORMS

SAMPLE ADDENDUM TO LEASE (LEASE OPTION)

The following is an example of an addendum I have used before. All options are negotiable. You will negotiate the option that is most compatible with your particular situation. This addendum is presented as an example only.

ADDENDUM TO LEASE

The following addendum applies to the attached lease:

(1)   At the completion of the first year's lease, if lessee purchases the property as described, security deposit will be applied to the last month's lease payment, or be applied to the down payment,

(2)   Lessor will allow a credit of $ ___DOLLAR AMOUNT____ per month from lease payment applied to any cash down payment, (or could be a percentage of the lease payment, i.e. "20% of any lease payments"), and

(3)   On or before ____DATE____ Lessor/owner agrees to sell to Lessee under an Agreement or Contract For Deed the property located at ___ADDRESS___ for the sum of ___DOLLAR AMOUNT__ payable as follows:

(a)   Lessee will pay an initial cash down payment of $ ___ DOLLAR AMOUNT ___.
        ($ ___ DOWN PAYMENT _____ less $ ___ DOLLAR AMOUNT _____ accrued through lease payments)

(b)   Owner will issue a Contract for Deed for the initial principal amount of $___ DOLLAR AMOUNT _____ amortized ___NUMBER OF YEARS ___ at a percentage of ___ PERCENTAGE RATE ___ (a cap statement can be added that states, "at a rate not to exceed __NUMBER OF PERCENTAGE POINTS __ above owner's mortgage at the time the Agreement for Deed is initiated.") Full payment (balloon) of principal will be due and payable ___NUMBER OF YEARS ___ years from date Contract for Deed is initiated. Mortgage will be adjusted to reflect any reductions in principal.

 Signatures:

Agreed: Lessor/Owner Date:

Agreed: Lessee Date:

SAMPLE AGREEMENT FOR DEED

The following is a sample Agreement for Deed. This form is presented as an example only.

AGREEMENT FOR DEED

ARTICLES OF AGREEMENT made this day of   19 , between   (SELLER) and   ,
husband and wife, (BUYER) WITNESSETH

THAT if the BUYER shall first make the payments and perform the covenants hereinafter
mentioned on their part to be made and performed, the SELLER hereby covenants and agree to
convey to the BUYER in fee simple absolute that parcel of land situated in the County of
State of   , known and described as follows:

Address   Lot ,   Block   ,as per plat thereof recorded in Plat Book, Pages through ,
Public Records of   County, State of

together with all appurtenances and hereditaments, thereof, but subject to all legal highways,
restrictions of record and zoning laws.

Also included in the sale of the above-described property are the following:

1.   The total purchase price for the said properly is   payable as follows:

a)   The sum of   as down payment has been paid by BUYER to SELLER;

b)   at the time of the full execution of this agreement, Buyers shall pay to Seller an additional
sum of ;

c)   the balance of the purchase price, namely   together with interest thereof at the rate
of   percent per annum, shall be payable in installments   per month plus escrow for
taxes and insurance commencing 30 (thirty) days from the execution of this agreement and
continuing on the 1st day of each month thereafter until the   when the entire outstanding
principal plus accrued interest, if any, shall be due and payable. Such payments shall be payable
to SELLER at   or at such other place or places as she may from time to time designate by
notice in writing. Each such installment when received by the SELLER, shall be credited first to
the payment of the interest on the then remaining unpaid principal balance of such purchase
price due to the date of the receipt of such installment, and then to the reduction of the unpaid
principal balance of such purchase price. The Buyer pay the cost of an insurance policy insuring
all buildings and improvements on said property for the full insurable value, including flood
insurance, with loss payable the SELLER, against loss by fire or other casualties and public
liability insurance on the property with limits of not less than $100, 000 per person and $300, 000
per accident throughout the term of this agreement.

2.   The SELLER, after the date of this agreement, shall not undertake any additional
improvements of perform any other work on said property which may result in the creation of
any mechanic's lien on said property without the written consent of the BUYER.

3.   All taxes, assessments pertaining to said property shall be prorated on the basis of the latest available bills as of 12:00 midnight on the day of

4.   The BUYER shall pay the cost of all utilities in connection with the property as they become due or payable on or after the date of this agreement.

5.   The BUYER agrees to maintain the property and the buildings and improvements thereon in as good order and repair as they are on the date of this agreement, reasonable wear and tear alone is excepted.

6.   The BUYER shall not remove or permit the removal from said property of any building or other improvement located thereon with first obtaining the written consent of the SELLER, nor shall the BUYER commit or permit be committed any waste of said property or any building or improvement thereon.

7.   The BUYER will not renovate, remodel or alter any building or improvement now or hereafter situated on said property, or construct any building, buildings, or improvements on said property without giving written notice and submitting plans for such renovating, remodeling or construction to the SELLER and first obtaining the SELLER'S approval in writing of such plans.

8.   The BUYER shall indemnify and hold the SELLER and the property of the SELLER, including the SELLER'S interest in said property, free and clear from liability for any and all mechanic's liens or other expense or damages resulting from any renovations, alterations, buildings, repair or other work placed on said property by the BUYER.

9.   The BUYER shall indemnify and hold the SELLER free and harmless from any and all demands, loss or resulting from the injury to, or death of, any person or persons because of negligence of the BUYER, or the conditions of said property at any time or times after the date of possession of said property is delivered to the BUYER.

10.   The BUYER will observe and obey all statutes , ordinances and laws of the United States, the State of and County of   . The BUYER will obey, all ordinances and laws with respect to the use and occupation of the property, will not do or suffer to be done anything that may constitute a nuisance.

11.   The BUYER shall be entitled to enter and to possession of said property on the
        and to continue in possession thereof so long as they are not in default in the performance of the AGREEMENT.

12.   The payments of all monies becoming due hereunder by the BUYER and the performance of all covenants and conditions of this agreement to be kept and performed by the BUYER are conditions precedent to the performance by the SELLER of the covenants and conditions of this agreement. to be kept and performed by the SELLER. In the event the BUYER shall fail for a period of thirty days after they become due to pay any of the sums of this agreement agreed to he paid by the BUYER, either installments on account of principal interest, taxes, assessments, or insurance premiums or should the BUYER fail to comply with any of the covenants or conditions of this AGREEMENT on her part to be performed, or if a receiver is appointed for the BUYER, or if the BUYER becomes bankrupt, or makes an assignment for the benefit of creditors, or should any action or proceeding be in any court to enforce any lien on, or claim against the property seeking to reach the interests of the BUYER, then;

a)   the SELLER shall be released from all obligations in law or equity to convey said property;

b)   the BUYER shall forfeit all rights to said property or to the possession thereof

c)   the SELLER shall have the immediate right to retake possession of said property;

d)   the payments heretofore made by the BUYER pursuant to this agreement shall be credited by the SELLER to the BUYER as reasonable rental value of said property during the period the BUYER had the use and occupancy of said property;

e)   the foregoing, the SELLER at their option, may declare, by notice to the BUYER that the entire unpaid balance of the purchase price specified in the AGREEMENT to be due and payable, and may by appropriate action in law or equity proceed to enforce payment thereof;

f)   any rights, powers or remedies, special, optional, or otherwise, given or reserved to the SELLER by this paragraph shall be construed to deprive the SELLER of any rights, powers; or remedies otherwise given by law or equity; and,

g)   if any action, negotiations, or other activity be brought by either party to enforce the terms, conditions and covenants of this agreement, then the defaulting party shall be liable to the non-defaulting party for expenses and cost, including reasonable attorneys' fees incurred through negotiation, trial, appeals, or otherwise, shall be borne by the defaulting party.

2.   When the purchase price and all other amount to be paid by the BUYER pursuant to this AGREEMENT are fully paid as provided for in this agreement, the SELLER execute and deliver to the BUYER a deed conveying good and marketable title to said property. Such conveyance shall be by statutory or general warranty deed free and clear of all encumbrances except easements, restrictions and limitations and conditions of record, not coupled with the possibility of reverter or right of reentry or other reverter right amounting a qualification of the fee, and subject to applicable zoning ordinances and real estate taxes for the year in which the deed is delivered and thereafter.

3.   Both BUYER and SELLER agree that this agreement constitutes the sole and only agreement between them respecting said property and correctly sets forth obligations to each other as of its date.

4.   Any and all notices or other communications required or allowed by this agreement or by law to be served or given to either party hereto by the other party shall be in writing, shall be deemed duly served when deposited: in the United States mail, first class postage addressed to BUYER at   or to the SELLERS at

5.   Either party may change their address for the purpose of this paragraph giving notice of such change to the other party in the manner provided herein.

6.   The parties agree to record this agreement in the Public Records of County,   State of

7.   This agreement shall be binding on and shall inure to the benefit of the heirs, executors, administrators, successors and assigns of the parties hereto, but nothing in this paragraph shall be construed as a consent by the SELLER to any assignment of the AGREEMENT or of any interest therein by the BUYER except as provided for below.

8.   Time is expressly declared to be the essence of this agreement.

9.   The waiver of any breach of this agreement by either of the parties shall not constitute a continuing waiver or a waiver of any subsequent breach, either of the same or of another provision of this agreement. The delay or omission by the SELLER to execute any right power , provided by this AGREEMENT shall not constitute a waiver of such right or power, or acquiescence in any default o! the part of the BUYER, nor shall be construed as a waiver or variation of the terms and conditions of this AGREEMENT . Any default on the BUYER shall be construed as continuous us, and the SELLER may exercise every right and power under his agreement at any time during the continuance of such default, or by the continuance of any subsequent default.

10.   The BUYER may make additional payments or the entire principal may be paid at any time, without charge or penalty.

11.   It is agreed by the BUYER and SELLER that this agreement shall be governed by the laws of the State of

IN WITNESS WHEREOF, We have hereunto set our hands and seals the day and year first above written.

Signed, seal and delivered in our presence:

SELLER: Date: (Name)

BUYER(S): [Names]   Date:

STATE OF COUNTY OF

I HEREBY CERTIFY that on this day, before me, an officer duly authorized in the State aforesaid and in the County aforesaid to take acknowledgment personally appeared

who executed the foregoing instrument and they acknowledged before me that they executed same.

WITNESS my hand and official seal in the, County, and State last aforesaid this day of 20XX NOTARY PUBLIC My Commission Expires:

A Summary of Your Rights Under the Fair Credit Reporting Act

The Federal Fair Credit Reporting Act (FCRA) is designed to promote accuracy, fairness, and privacy of information in the files of every "consumer-reporting agency" (CRA). Most CRAs are credit bureaus that gather and sell information about you -- such as if you pay your bills on time or have filed bankruptcy -- to creditors, employers, landlords, and other businesses. You can find the complete text of the FCRA, 15 U.S.C. §§1681-1681u. The FCRA gives you specific rights, as outlined below. You may have additional rights under state law. You may contact a state or local consumer protection agency or a state attorney general to learn those rights.

•   You must be told if information in your file has been used against you. Anyone who uses information from a CRA to take action against you -- such as denying an application for credit, insurance, or employment -- must tell you, and give you the name, address, and phone number of the CRA that provided the consumer report.

•   You can find out what is in your file. At your request, a CRA must give you the information in your file, and a list of everyone who has requested it recently. There is no charge for the report if a person has taken action against you because of information supplied by the CRA, if you request the report within 60 days of receiving notice of the action. You also are entitled to one free report every twelve months upon request if you certify that (1) you are unemployed and plan to seek employment within 60 days, (2) you are on welfare, or (3) your report is inaccurate due to fraud. Otherwise, a CRA may charge you up to eight dollars.

•   You can dispute inaccurate information with the CRA. If you tell a CRA that your file contains inaccurate information, the CRA must investigate the items (usually within 30 days) by presenting to its information source all relevant evidence you submit, unless your dispute is frivolous. The source must review your evidence and report its findings to the CRA. (The source also must advise national CRAs -- to which it has provided the data -- of any error.) The CRA must give you a written report of the investigation, and a copy of your report if the investigation results in any change. If the CRA's investigation does not resolve the dispute, you may add a brief statement to your file. The CRA must normally include a summary of your statement in future reports. If an item is deleted or a dispute statement is filed, you may ask that anyone who has recently received your report be notified of the change.

• Inaccurate information must be corrected or deleted. A CRA must remove or correct inaccurate or unverified information from its files, usually within 30 days after you dispute it. However, the CRA is not required to remove accurate data from your file unless it is outdated (as described below) or cannot be verified. If your dispute results in any change to your report, the CRA cannot reinsert into your file a disputed item unless the information source verifies its accuracy and completeness. In addition, the CRA must give you a written notice telling you it has reinserted the item. The notice must include the name, address and phone number of the information source.

• You can dispute inaccurate items with the source of the information. If you tell anyone -- such as a creditor who reports to a CRA -- that you dispute an item, they may not then report the information to a CRA without including a notice of your dispute. In addition, once you've notified the source of the error in writing, it may not continue to report the information if it is, in fact, an error.

• Outdated information may not be reported. In most cases, a CRA may not report negative information that is more than seven years old; ten years for bankruptcies.

• Access to your file is limited. A CRA may provide information about you only to people with a need recognized by the FCRA -- usually to consider an application with a creditor, insurer, employer, landlord, or other business.

• Your consent is required for reports that are provided to employers, or reports that contain medical information. A CRA may not give out information about you to your employer, or prospective employer, without your written consent. A CRA may not report medical information about you to creditors, insurers, or employers without your permission.

• You may choose to exclude your name from CRA lists for unsolicited credit and insurance offers. Creditors and insurers may use file information as the basis for sending you unsolicited offers of credit or insurance. Such offers must include a toll-free phone number for you to call if you want your name and address removed from future lists. If you call, you must be kept off the lists for two years. If you request, complete, and return the CRA form provided for this purpose, you must be taken off the lists indefinitely.

• You may seek damages from violators. If a CRA, a user or (in some cases) a provider of CRA data, violates the FCRA, you may sue them in state or federal court.

Made in the USA
Middletown, DE
11 November 2021